The
Best Way Out
is Always
Through

THE POWER OF PERSEVERANCE

BJ Gallagher

Published by Simple Truths, LLC
1952 McDowell Road, Suite 300
Naperville, IL 60563

Design: Rich Nickel
Edited by: Stephanie Trannel
Photo credits: Getty Images, Bruce Heinemann, Jerry Park, SR Marquis, Steve Terrill, Rich Nickel and Jeff Vanuga

Printed and bound in the United States of America

www.simpletruths.com
(800) 900-3427

06WOZ 13

How do you get through tough times?

Introduction

"Have you always been a writer?" people often ask when we first meet. Many assume that I've been a successful author my whole life. Nothing could be further from the truth.

Years ago, I was a teenage bride with an infant son, working a low-paying clerical job to help my 21-year-old husband through college. Immaturity took its toll on our marriage and we divorced before our son was three. I moved in with my mom and dad for a year, and took a job working nights as a waitress while my mother cared for my baby.

I didn't start college until I was 23, living in a damp basement apartment with my four-year-old toddler. I carried a full class load and earned good grades, while trying to be a good mother, too. It was lonely and hard being a full-time student and a single mom. While other girls were going to parties and football games with handsome frat boys, I was making peanut butter and jelly sandwiches, teaching my son how to ride a bicycle, reading him bedtime stories, and bandaging his skinned knees.

Since then, my life and career have taken many turns, many of them difficult. Over the years, I've struggled with self-doubt and single-parent guilt, wishing my son Michael didn't have to be a latch-key kid. I wanted to give him all the advantages in life, but couldn't.

I've dealt with alcoholic family members, the divorce of my parents, and the care of elderly loved ones. My son and I have had our share of illnesses, injuries, car accidents, and loss. Tough times and personal challenges have come in many forms, with many faces.

And through it all, the single most important thing that has helped me survive — no, thrive — is perseverance. The person I am today is a testament to the power of patience, perseverance and faith. I am an ordinary person who has been blessed with extraordinary success by simply sticking with it.

I hope that this book will help you find your own inner strength to keep on keeping on — no matter what challenges life brings.

* * *

Nothing in this world can take the place of **persistence.** Talent will not; nothing is more common than unsuccessful people with talent. Genius will not; unrewarded genius is almost a proverb. Education will not; the world is full of educated derelicts. Persistence and determination alone are omnipotent. The slogan, **"Press on,"** has solved, and always will solve, the problems of the human race.

• Calvin Coolidge, 30th President of the U.S.

My learning disability gave me certain advantages, because I was able to **live in the moment** and **capitalize on opportunities** I spotted.

• Paul Orfalea, founder of Kinko's

How do you get through tough times?

Persist no matter what.

P
E
R
S
E
V
E
R
E

Overcoming Personal Limitations

"Kinko" they nicknamed him as a kid, referring to his head of wild, curly, red hair. But teasing about his kinky hair was the least of his problems. Paul Orfalea struggled with severe dyslexia and ADHD: he flunked second grade twice, graduated from high school at the bottom of his class, and eked through college with a "C" average. He had a hard time sitting still, and could barely read or write. No one ever voted him "most likely to succeed."

Paul applied for jobs and managed to get hired twice — but neither job lasted longer than a day. It was clear he wasn't cut out for traditional employment in a 9-to-5 world. He knew he was different and that somehow he'd have to find his own way in the world.

In 1970, living in a small college town near Santa Barbara, California, Paul noticed that there were always long lines at the copy machines. "Too many students and not enough copiers," he thought to himself. So he borrowed $5000 and opened his own copier business in a tiny little 9x12 foot storefront close to campus. His space was so small that he had to move the copy machine out to the sidewalk to use it. He hawked pens and pencils from his backpack as he stood outside drumming up business.

People told Paul he was crazy, but he'd been hearing that his whole life so he just ignored them. He knew his idea was a good one and he had the determination, energy, and persistence to pursue it despite what anyone said.

He worked long and hard, and within a year, he had made enough money to expand. Ten years later, there were 80 Kinko's stores in college towns all around the country. In another ten years (1990) that number expanded exponentially to 420 stores. Just seven years later the number of stores doubled again to 840!

This curly-headed kid with severe learning disabilities had built himself a hugely successful business simply by seeing a need and filling it. He understood his limitations, so he hired great people to do all the things he couldn't. He was the idea man — he hired others to execute his plans.

Paul Orfalea went on to establish the Orfalea Family Foundation to support causes he's passionate about, and in 2005 coauthored a successful book to share his story and inspire others with learning disabilities *(Copy This! Lessons from a hyperactive dyslexic who turned a bright idea into one of America's best companies).*

Finally, in 2004, Paul sold Kinko's to FedEx for $2.4 billion. Not bad for a guy who can't read or write very well.

Nothing in life just happens.

You have to have the stamina to meet the obstacles and overcome them.

• Golda Meir, Fourth Prime Minister of Israel

If everybody else is doing it one way, there's a good chance you can find your niche by **going in exactly the opposite direction.** But be prepared for a lot of folks to wave you down and tell you you're headed the wrong way.

• Sam Walton, founder of Wal-Mart and Sam's Club

Success is to be measured not so much by the position that one has reached in life as by the **obstacles which they have overcome.**

• Booker T. Washington, freed from slavery as a child,
he gained an education, was appointed to lead a college
for blacks, and became a national leader of the
African American community

Swimming
Upstream
by BJ Gallagher

Sometimes you feel like a salmon
swimming upstream.
It takes **all your strength**
to fight the current
that tries to drag you down.

But you resist –
you persist.
You keep going
onward and upward.

There are rocks in your way –
sometimes pebbles,
sometimes boulders.
So you swim around,
jump over,
wriggle under
any which way you can.

You keep going
onward and upward.

The current is swift and cold,
the water turbulent.
Sometimes it seems hopeless,
fruitless,
pointless.
Your strength ebbs,
your energy flags,
but still **you persist.**

You keep going
*onward
and
upward.*

When you come to
the end of your rope,
tie a knot and
hang on.

• Franklin D. Roosevelt, 32nd President of the U.S.

Tips for Tough Times

The only way out is *through*.
Some days you can move through
difficulties quickly; other days
it feels as if you're
slogging through Jell-O.
Don't look too far ahead or
you'll get overwhelmed.
Just do the next apparent thing.
Keep putting one foot
in front of the other.
You'll get through this.
And when you do, *you'll feel great!*

If what I feel were equally distributed
to the whole human family, there would
not be one cheerful face on earth.

• Abraham Lincoln, 16th President of the U.S.

How do you get through tough times?

P
Endure discomfort.
R
S
E
V
E
R
E

Working Through Depression & Disappointment

Many people do not know that Abe Lincoln, one of the best Presidents we've ever had, endured many hardships and heartaches throughout the course of his life — at times struggling with severe depression. Consider the following:

- He spent his childhood working on the family farm, with long days of back-breaking toil. Unfortunate circumstances forced his family to abandon their home in Kentucky, and move across the river to Indiana, in search of better opportunities.

- His mother died when he was just ten years old, leaving his father to raise the children.

- He went to work for a none-too-scrupulous businessman who ran the business into the ground, leaving young Abe unemployed.

- He ran for the Illinois state legislature and lost, finishing eighth in a field of thirteen.

- He signed a note to buy into a general store with a friend, but within a year they were out of business, overwhelmed by a better-organized competitor in the same town.

- He fell in love with Ann Rutledge, became engaged to marry her, only to have her die unexpectedly. He was heartbroken and severely depressed.

- He fell in love again and married Mary Todd. Together they had four sons, three of whom died before reaching adulthood.

- He was finally successful in getting elected to the state legislature and made two attempts to become speaker. He was defeated both times.

- He wanted to run for Congress but failed to achieve his party's nomination.

- He ultimately won a seat in Congress. But when he sought to run for the U.S. Senate, he couldn't muster the votes and withdrew from the election.

- He was selected as a Vice Presidential candidate, but due to late entry in the field, he couldn't win enough votes.

- He ran for the Senate again but didn't win the seat because his party failed to gain control of the legislature.

But despite all the struggles and setbacks, at no point did Lincoln ever give up; personally or professionally. He endured great pain and sadness, but he didn't let it stop him. He just kept going.

Finally, he ran for the highest office in the land and became the 16th President of the United States at a time when our country was facing its worst internal crisis ever: the Civil War. Lincoln won the war, ended slavery, and unified the nation.

If ever there was a man who exemplified perseverance and the enduring of personal discomfort, it was Abraham Lincoln. If he could have such pain in his life and still achieve all that he did, how can you – how can I – let discomfort stop us from achieving our own goals?

It takes **courage to push yourself** to places that you have never been before ... to test your limits ... to break through barriers. And the day came when the risk it took to remain tight inside the bud was more painful than the risk it took to blossom.

• Anaïs Nin, French diarist

The last three or four reps is what makes the muscle grow. This area of pain **divides the champion from someone else** who is not a champion. That's what most people lack, having the guts to go on and just say they'll go through the pain no matter what happens.

• Arnold Schwarzenegger, champion bodybuilder, action movie star, Governor of California

If you want to increase your success rate, **double your failure rate.**

• Thomas Watson Sr., founding president of IBM

Character cannot be developed in ease and quiet. Only through **experience of trial and suffering** can the soul be strengthened, vision cleared, ambition inspired, and success achieved.

• Helen Keller, first deaf blind person to earn a college degree, author, activist

It Only Hurts When I *Laugh*

by BJ Gallagher

Nobody ever promised you
a rose garden,
but who knew
the thorns would be so sharp?

Tough times are painful –
your head hurts,
your back aches,
your heart breaks.
Sometimes everything seems to hurt.

When will it end?
Or will it ever end?

Discomfort and pain
are easier to bear
when you know
they're not permanent.
But it's harder
when there's no end in sight.

Hang in there, now.
Remember to breathe.

Nothing is forever,
and this too shall pass.
Watch for that light
at the end of the tunnel …
and pray that it's *not a train!*

Challenges are gifts that force us to search for a new center of gravity. Don't fight them. Just find a *different* way to stand.

• Oprah Winfrey, talk show host, media entrepreneur

Tips for Tough Times

What would radical self care look like for you?
How can you take good care of yourself
during difficult times?

- **Be kind and gentle with yourself.**
- **Rest and *restore your energy* as often as you need to.**
- **Eat simple, healthy foods.**
- **Listen to *soothing* music.**
- **Drink lots of water.**
- **Do the spiritual things that *comfort and nurture* you.**

Some people fold after making one timid request. They quit too soon. **Keep asking** until you find the answers. In sales, there are usually four or five "nos" before you get a "yes."

• Jack Canfield, coauthor of the *Chicken Soup for the Soul* series of books

How do you get through tough times?

P E R S E V E R E

Request help from other people.

Searching for "Yes" in the Land of "No"

Millions of people say that they'd like to write a book someday — a novel, their life story, a children's book, a murder mystery, or perhaps a self-help book. Of these millions, perhaps a million of them actually do it in any given year. Of this million, almost 300,000 of them get published (in 2007 the figure was 291,922). Each of these books has less than a 1% chance of being stocked in an average bookstore, and the average book sells about 500 copies. *(Publishers Weekly, 2006)* In other words, once you write a book, getting it published is a long shot. And if you get it published, making it successful is an even bigger long shot.

Jack Canfield and Mark Victor Hansen learned this the hard way. They spent three years gathering stories and editing them for a collection they called *Happy Little Stories.* By the time they were finished, they were $140,000 in debt.

Then they found a literary agent who agreed to represent them and he set about sending the manuscript to publishers he thought might be interested. The response was unanimous: "no." One publisher said, "Nobody buys anthologies anymore." Another said, "It's not topical enough." Yet another said, "We just don't get it."

And finally, the worst "no" of all — their literary agent dropped them. After pitching the book to dozens of publishers he came up empty-handed. "I can't sell this book," he told them. "Nobody buys short stories."

That could have been the end of the story for Canfield and Hansen. Undoubtedly, most authors would have given up by now; but not these two. Instead, they decided to try to sell the book themselves.

They made 200 copies of their manuscript, stuffed them into their backpacks, and headed to the annual American Bookseller's Association convention (now called Book Expo America). They roamed the aisles of the huge convention center, button-holing every editor and publisher they could find. They handed out dozens of copies of their manuscript, but still no takers.

Finally, after two days of non-stop hunting and schmoozing, they met Peter Vegso, owner of a small publishing house in Deerfield Beach, Florida called Health Communications, Inc. (HCI). This publisher was in the business of doing primarily recovery books (12-step), but they had fallen on hard times, as the recovery movement peaked and waned. On the verge of bankruptcy, Vegso had put his company on the market to sell it.

In the meantime, he was still trying desperately to save it by expanding into a broader category of spiritual books. Vegso agreed to take a chance on this collection of happy stories. After all, he figured, he didn't have much to lose.

After much discussion, they changed the name of the book to *Chicken Soup for the Soul,* and in 1993 HCI published it. Then the hard work for the authors began in earnest. As Hansen says today, "Making your book successful is five percent about writing a good book, and ninety-five percent marketing."

He knows what he's talking about. He and Canfield lived it. For the first year after the book was published, both men lived, breathed, ate, and slept their book. They were monomaniacs with a mission. They had bet the farm on their book — mortgaging their houses to the hilt — working non-stop, day and night, to make their baby successful.

They went to their hometown newspaper, the *Los Angeles Times,* and walked through the newsroom one afternoon, handing out copies of *Chicken Soup* to every reporter and editor, hoping that someone would write about their book. No one did.

They spread the word: sending out press releases, doing book signings, promoting their book during their seminars and workshops, and hiring publicists and others to help them make their book successful.

Canfield and Hansen did everything they could to take their baby to the top, and in fourteen months they made it. They arrived at the Nirvana of books and authors — the #1 spot on the *New York Times* Best-seller list — where they remained for two years.

The authors were winners and so was their publisher! Together they accomplished the "impossible." Vegso saved his publishing company from bankruptcy and the authors made their dream come true.

As of January 2006, there were over 105 titles in the *Chicken Soup* series of books, with over 100 million copies in print in 54 languages.

Canfield and Hansen are living proof of the power in asking for what you want, seeking out help from others, and refusing to take "no" for an answer. They knew that all they needed was ONE "yes" to get the book published, so they just kept going through all the "nos" until they found it.

* * *

None of us got where we are solely by pulling ourselves up by our bootstraps. We got here because **somebody bent down and helped us pick up our boots.**

• Thurgood Marshall, first black Justice of the U.S. Supreme Court

What do we live for, if not to make life less difficult for each other?

• George Eliot (Mary Ann Evans), English writer who wrote under a male pen name

Three of the most powerful words in the English language are: **"Please help me."**

• Cathy Conheim, therapist and coauthor of *What's the Matter with Henry? The True Tale of a Three-legged Cat*

In prosperity our friends know us; in adversity **we know our friends.**

• John Churton Collins, British literary critic

Do not save your loving speeches for your friends till they are dead.
Do not write them on their tombstones; **speak them now** instead.

• Anna Cummins, author

S.O.S.
(Sharing Our Struggles)

by BJ Gallagher

No one can do it for you
but you can't do it alone.

We all have difficulties,
challenges,
problems to bear.

We can't ask someone else
to take them from us,
for they already have their own.

But we can ask them
to help us –
to share our burdens and trials.

And we, in turn,
can do the same
for them.

Together we shift and share
our struggle and
troubles ...
lightening the burden
by lifting the load
on many shoulders.

A community is greater
than the sum of its
individuals.

Our synergy multiplies
our strength,
and *together*
we can handle
almost anything.

When a friend is in trouble, don't annoy him by asking if there is anything you can do. Think up something appropriate and **do it.**

• Edgar Watson Howe, novelist, journalist, editor

Tips for Tough Times

That which is sharable is bearable.

Who do you turn to when the burden is too much to carry alone? A family member, a spiritual advisor, a trusted friend, a close confidante … or all of these?

In asking for help, you are giving people the opportunity to contribute to you. In so doing, you honor them as well.

I think that somehow **we learn who we really are** and then live with that decision.

• Eleanor Roosevelt, First Lady, social activist, U.N. delegate

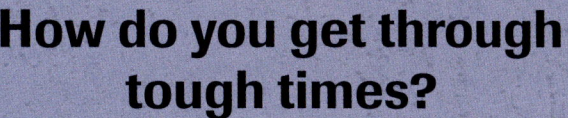

How do you get through tough times?

P
E
R
Steadfastly hold on to your beliefs and values.
E
V
E
R
E

The Ugly Duckling

Although Eleanor Roosevelt was born into the lap of luxury in New York City — part of a high society known as the "swells" — she was not a happy little girl. Insecure and starved for affection, she thought herself to be ugly and ungraceful. Her mother Anna didn't help her daughter's poor self-image, telling guests that Eleanor was "such a funny child, so old-fashioned, we always call her Granny."

Anna Roosevelt died of diphtheria when Eleanor was just eight, so she and her two brothers were sent to live with their maternal grandmother. Her father Elliot died of alcoholism two years later, just before Eleanor turned ten.

At age 15, she was sent off to finishing school in England. There, she gained a bit of confidence, learned to speak fluent French, and thrived under the tutelage of a feminist headmistress who was committed to teaching her girls to think for themselves.

At 17, Eleanor returned to the U.S., ending her formal education. She was given a debutante party to mark her entrance into society, as was customary for young ladies of that era and social class. Shortly thereafter, she met a distant cousin, young Franklin Delano Roosevelt, who was a student at Harvard, and their courtship began.

Franklin married Eleanor when she was 19, beginning what would be a long and challenging marriage. Franklin's domineering mother, Sara, bullied the young bride, who was still struggling with insecurity and self-doubt. Sara wanted to help the motherless girl, but the relationship proved difficult, especially for Eleanor. Sara had always doted on her son and was determined that he be successful in life; she made it her business to mold his new bride into a suitable wife.

Eleanor bore Franklin six children in the first ten years of marriage, one of whom died in infancy. Her hands full with her brood, Eleanor had little time for, or interest in, her husband's political career. She let her mother-in-law dominate their family life in these early years of her marriage, feeling the need for the older woman's experience and advice.

But all that changed in the summer of 1921, their sixteenth year together. Franklin came down with a high fever while they were summering on Campobello Island, off the coast of Maine. The doctors said it was polio; Franklin's legs were permanently paralyzed.

Sara was devastated by her beloved son's illness and wanted to baby and pamper him. Eleanor, strengthened by the crisis, stood up to Sara and refused to let her husband become an invalid. She devoted herself to nursing him back to health and encouraged his political aspirations.

Eleanor began filling in for her husband at public appearances. She got involved with the Women's Trade Union League, raising money for the union's goals: a 48-hour work week, minimum wage, and the abolishment of child labor. She was getting a taste of the social and political activism that would grow to dominate her later years. Throughout the '20s she became increasingly influential in the Democratic Party of New York. She campaigned for Alfred E. Smith to become President and her husband to become Governor of New York. Smith lost, but Roosevelt won.

Franklin's political career progressed, and so did Eleanor's self-confidence. She was no longer the brow-beaten daughter-in-law of Sara Roosevelt — she had become her own woman.

When Franklin won the White House in 1933, Eleanor knew that she was going to be a different type of First Lady than her predecessors. She continued with speaking engagements and social activism, despite criticism from those who insisted that a woman's place is in the home. She started holding weekly press conferences, the first First Lady to do so. Eleanor began writing a syndicated newspaper column, and made personal appearances at labor meetings to reassure workers that the White House was not insensitive to their plight during the Depression. She saw herself as a human link between government bureaucracy and the citizens who so needed government's help.

This pioneering First Lady spoke out in support of the early civil rights movement of African-Americans. She resigned her membership in the Daughters of the American Revolution in 1939 when they refused to allow black singer Marian Anderson perform in Constitution Hall. She helped arrange a subsequent concert for the singer on the steps of the Lincoln Memorial.

Eleanor accomplished much in her twelve years in the White House, and she continued her activism after Franklin died in 1945. She served as a delegate to the United Nations from 1946 to 1953, and was the first chairperson of the U.N. Human Rights Commission. In 1961, President John F. Kennedy appointed a new "President's Commission on the Status of Women" with Eleanor as its first chairwoman.

Eleanor's personal life was as challenging, or more so, than her public life. Her husband's affair with Lucy Mercer nearly destroyed her marriage and family. Despite the fact that Franklin vowed to end the affair, he and Lucy continued their romance for the last fifteen years of his life, including his entire time as President. Many scholars have suggested that it was Franklin's infidelity — not his illness — that fueled Eleanor's newfound independence and strength. She emerged from that crisis with the awareness that fulfillment could only come through her own influence and life, not someone else's.

Eleanor's life exemplifies one of her most famous quotes:

"A woman is like a tea bag — you never know how strong she is until she gets in hot water."

Never give in! Never give in! Never, never, never, never — in nothing great or small, large or petty. **Never give in** except to convictions of honor and good sense.

• Sir Winston Churchill, British statesman and Prime Minister during WWII

Never confuse a single defeat with a **final** defeat.

• F. Scott Fitzgerald, author of *The Great Gatsby*

You come to the planet with nothing and you leave with nothing, so you'd better **do some good** while you're here.

• Alex Van Halen, member of the band Van Halen, inducted into the Rock and Roll Hall of Fame in 2007

Where Is Your True North?

by BJ Gallagher

There aren't many things in life
that are *really* yours…
Possessions and things,
they come and go.
Material objects,
which seem so substantial,
are instead ephemeral,
ultimately decay and turn to dust.

It's the *intangible* things
that are the most enduring and real —
integrity,
values,
character,
friendship and love.

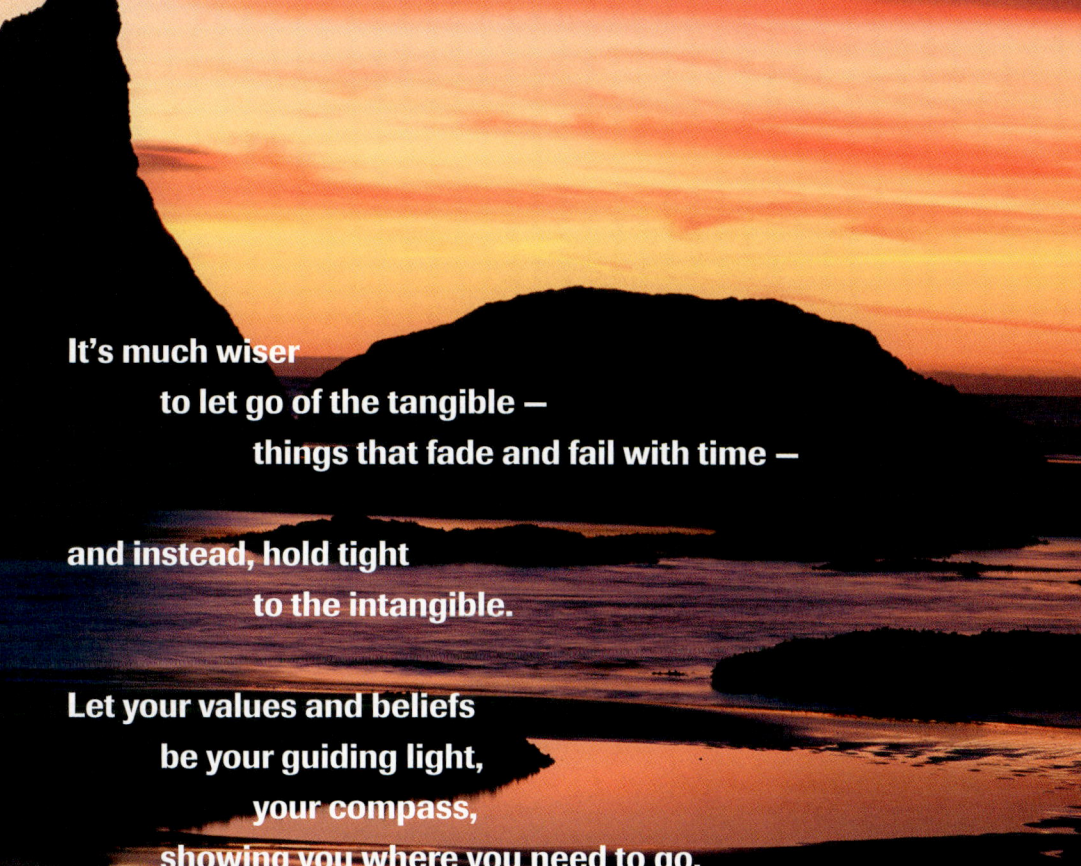

It's much wiser
  to let go of the tangible —
    things that fade and fail with time —

and instead, hold tight
  to the intangible.

Let your values and beliefs
  be your guiding light,
    your compass,
    showing you where you need to go.

Stay the course —
  aim for the True North
    of your heart.

We don't see things as they are; we see things **as we are.**

• Anaïs Nin, French diarist

Tips for Tough Times

Make a list of the five most important values you hold dear.

Things like health, family, creativity, achievement, travel, community, spirituality, serving others, play or others.

List these five things on sticky notes and place them where you will see them often. They will serve to remind you to spend your time, energy and money in keeping with your values.

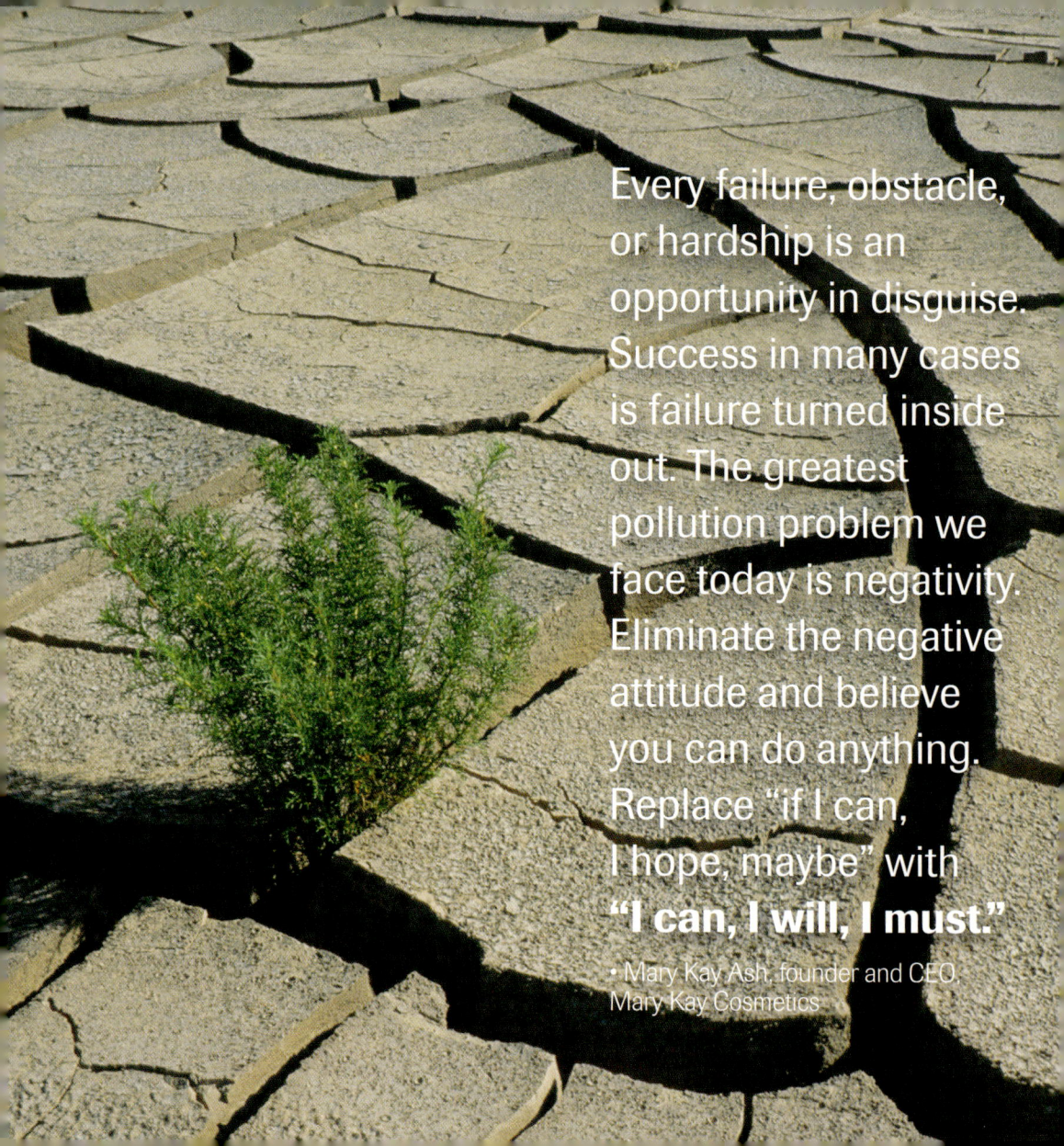

Every failure, obstacle, or hardship is an opportunity in disguise. Success in many cases is failure turned inside out. The greatest pollution problem we face today is negativity. Eliminate the negative attitude and believe you can do anything. Replace "if I can, I hope, maybe" with **"I can, I will, I must."**

• Mary Kay Ash, founder and CEO, Mary Kay Cosmetics

How do you get through tough times?

P
E
R
S
E
V
E
R
E

PERSEnvision triumph.

Driving the Road to Success in a Pink Cadillac

Mary Kay Ash banged her head on the corporate glass ceiling one too many times. Working for several direct sales companies from the 1930s until the early 1960s, she achieved considerable success. She climbed the corporate ladder to become the sole woman on the board of directors of the World Gift Company — quite an accomplishment for a woman in the 1950s.

But life wasn't rosy at the top. Even though Mary Kay had the title and the track record, she was not taken seriously by her male peers. In board meetings, her opinions and suggestions were ignored, dismissed, or even ridiculed. Male board members minced no words in their judgment, pronouncing her guilty of "thinking like a woman."

Since the sales force was almost entirely female, Mary Kay thought that thinking like a woman was an asset . But her fellow board members disagreed. Finally, in frustration, she retired in 1963, intending to write a book to assist women in the male-dominated business.

Sitting at her kitchen table, she made two lists: one list was all the good things she had seen in the companies where she'd worked, and the other list was all the things she thought could be improved. As she re-read her lists, she realized that what she had in front of her was a marketing plan for her ideal company. In just four weeks, her "book" had become a business plan, and her retirement was over.

Both her accountant and her attorney did their best to discourage her, warning that she would be throwing her money away on this venture. But Mary Kay had heard enough male nay-saying in her corporate years — she ignored her advisors.

Her husband, unlike her accountant and attorney, was very supportive. With his help, Mary Kay developed cosmetic products, designed packaging, wrote promotional materials and recruited and trained her female sales force.

Then the unthinkable happened; her husband of twenty-one years died of a heart attack. Another woman might have dropped her plans, or at least delayed them, but Mary Kay was a strong Texas woman. She stayed on track with the help of her twenty-year-old son, Richard Rogers, and rolled out her new business in September of 1963.

Beginning with a storefront in Dallas and an investment of $5,000, Mary Kay Cosmetics earned close to $200,000 in its first year — quadrupling that amount in its second year. When Mary Kay took her company public in 1968, sales had climbed to more than $10 million.

Mary Kay understood human motivation and the importance of recognition better than any CEO of her time. She designed an incentive program that was virtually unlimited, enabling her sales consultants to make as much money as their talent and ambition could earn them. Awarding pink Cadillacs to top sales people was a touch of pure genius, for nothing says "I'm successful" quite like cruising down the highway in a rose-colored Caddy.

Mary Kay's unusual corporate motto, "God first, family second, career third," was unconventional, to say the least. But she understood the need for women to have balance in their lives, and she was committed to providing unlimited opportunity for women's financial AND personal success.

Mary Kay authored three books, all of which became best-sellers. Her business model is taught at the Harvard Business School. She received many honors, including the Horatio Alger Award. Fortune magazine has named Mary Kay Cosmetics as one of the Ten Best Companies for Women, as well as one of The 100 Best Companies to Work for in America.

At the time of her death in 2001, Mary Kay Cosmetics had 800,000 independent beauty consultants in 37 countries, with total annual sales of over two billion dollars. Never underestimate the power of a woman with a mission!

The thing always
happens that you
really believe in;
and the belief in
a thing makes
it happen.

• Frank Lloyd Wright, architect

The very least you can do in your life is to figure out what you hope for. And the most you can do is **live inside that hope.** Not admire it from a distance but live right in it, under its roof.

• Barbara Kingsolver, author

A Vision
of Beauty

by BJ Gallagher

Picture it.

Hold the image in your mind,
the vision in your heart.

You'll see it
when you believe it —
not the other way around.

All great human achievements
started off as an idea,
a picture in
someone's head.

Your achievement,
your goal,
your fulfillment,
your future
are like postcards
tacked to the bulletin board
of your mind.

Keep them visible —
look at them often.

See yourself in those pictures
and know that dreams
really do come true.

Dream as if you'll live forever.

Live as if you'll die tomorrow.

• James Dean, actor

Tips for Tough Times

The human mind thinks in pictures.

Having visual images of your dreams, goals and heart's desire helps manifest them in your life.

Paint a picture in your mind. Create a movie in your head. Play that movie again and again.

You are the star in your own life!

Dedication, **absolute dedication,** is what keeps one ahead – a sort of indomitable obsessive dedication and the realization that there is no end or limit to this because life is simply an ever-growing process, an ever-renewing process.

• Bruce Lee, Kung Fu master and movie star

How do you get through tough times?

P
E
R
S
E
Very consistently
keep at it.
E
R
E

Kung Fu Fighting Through Barriers and Bias

Show business is brutally difficult, especially if you're not a classically handsome, caucasian, leading man kind of guy like Clarke Gable, John Wayne, Michael Douglas, George Clooney or Brad Pitt. Martial artist Bruce Lee knew that, but would not be deterred from his dream of becoming the biggest Chinese star in the world.

His birth was auspicious. He came into this world in the Hour of the Dragon (between 6 and 8am), in the Year of the Dragon, 1940, according to the Chinese zodiac calendar. It doesn't get any better than dragons in Chinese cosmology.

Born Lee Jun Fan in San Francisco's Chinatown, he was also given the English name "Bruce" by a physician at the hospital, though his family never called him that. He was automatically a United States citizen by virtue of his birth in the U.S., but his parents were not. His father, Lee Hoi-Chuen, and his mother Grace, moved back to Hong Kong with their infant son when he was three months old.

Bruce Lee's father was a famous Cantonese Opera star who introduced his son to the world of performing at a very early age. His first role was as a baby carried onto the stage by an actor. Young Lee appeared in several black-and-white short films, and by the time he was 18 he had appeared in twenty films.

Lee attended private boys' schools in Hong Kong, learning English along with all the other subjects a well-educated young man needs to learn. Strong and athletic, he was a skillful boxer who represented his schools in tournaments.

At age 18 he got into a serious fight with another young man, beating his opponent badly, resulting in police involvement. Fearing for his son's safety, Lee Hoi-Chuen sent Bruce back to San Francisco to live with a family friend. He left Hong Kong with $100 in his pocket and two titles: 1958 Boxing Champion and the Crown Cha Cha Champion of Hong Kong.

He stayed in San Francisco for awhile, then moved to Seattle, Washington, to work for another family friend. After finishing high school in 1959, he went on to Edison Technical School where he earned his diploma, finally enrolling in the University of Washington where he studied drama, psychology and other subjects. It was at university that he met his future wife, Linda Emery, whom he married in 1964.

During these early years in the U.S., Lee abandoned any idea of a film career in favor of pursuing martial arts. But Hollywood beckoned in 1964 when, at a high-profile martial arts demonstration at the Long Beach Karate Tournament, he was seen by someone who worked for William Dozier, the producer of *Batman*. Dozier invited Lee to an audition, where his lightning-fast moves so impressed the producers that they cast Lee in the sidekick role of Kato on the TV series *The Green Hornet.* Lee was sure that this was his big break, but the show was cancelled after just one season in 1967.

Compounding his frustration, Lee injured his back after failing to warm up properly during a workout session. His doctors prescribed bed rest for several months and suggested he abandon martial arts altogether.

Lee accepted the former, but rejected the latter advice. For the next six months, he stayed flat on his back, letting his injury heal. But while his body was resting his mind was busy. He started making notes about his martial arts methods, thinking about everything he had learned so far. By the time he was up and around again his notes filled eight volumes. Included is this affirmation:

"I, Bruce Lee, will be the highest paid Oriental superstar in the U.S. In return, I will give the most exciting performances and render the best quality in the capacity of an actor. Starting in 1970, I will achieve world fame and from then onward till the end of 1980 I will have in my possession $10,000,000. Then I will live the way I please and achieve inner harmony and happiness."

Lee made a number of appearances in small roles on various television shows, and in one movie, *Marlowe,* where he delighted audiences by trashing Marlowe's office with leaping kicks and flashing punches. He appeared as a martial arts instructor in four segments of the 1971 TV series *Longstreet* and later tried to pitch a TV series of his own titled *The Warrior.* Warner Brothers retooled Lee's ideas and named the series *Kung Fu,* about a Shaolin monk in the Wild West. The lead role was given to a non-martial artist, actor David Carradine, because studio execs thought that the American public would not accept a Chinese leading man.

Fed up with being rejected because of his race, Lee accepted a film contract by legendary Hong Kong director, Raymond Chow, who promised to make the martial artist a star. Good to his word, he cast Lee as the leading man in *The Big Boss,* which became a huge success across Asia, catapulting Lee to stardom. Chow and Lee followed up with two more major successes in 1972: *Fist of Fury* and *Way of the Dragon.* With *Dragon,* Lee was more than just the star – he was also writing, directing and choreographing all the fight scenes. He was well on his way to achieving his dream of being an international superstar.

He didn't have to wait long. The very next year, 1973, Raymond Chow's production company teamed up with Warner Brothers to produce *Enter the Dragon* – the first film ever co-produced by Chinese and American studios. To date, it has grossed over $200 million. Its success, both in the U.S. and in Europe, established Bruce Lee as an international movie star and martial arts legend.

Dragons are indeed auspicious in Chinese culture. And with *Enter the Dragon,* Bruce Lee — born in the Hour of the Dragon in the Year of the Dragon — finally fulfilled his destiny,

Sadly, Lee died suddenly and mysteriously just a few months after completing production on the movie, and just three weeks before it was released. But he is still considered the greatest martial artist of the 20th century.

* * *

It's not that I'm so smart – it's just that I stay with problems longer.

• Albert Einstein, German-born, Nobel Prize-winning physicist (Theory of Relativity and Quantum Physics)

I think a hero is an ordinary individual who finds the **strength to persevere** and endure in spite of overwhelming obstacles.

• Christopher Reeve, *Superman* actor, became paralyzed from the neck down due to a spinal cord injury

All that is necessary to break the spell of inertia and frustration is this: **act as if it were impossible to fail.** That is the talisman, the formula, the command of right-about-face which turns us from failure towards success.

• Dorothea Brande, author, editor

There are **no shortcuts** to any place worth going.

• Beverly Sills, opera star

I don't know anything about luck. I've never banked on it, and I'm afraid of people who do. Luck to me is something else: **hard work** and realizing what is opportunity and what isn't.

• Lucille Ball, comedy actor, star of *I Love Lucy*

Staying the Course

by BJ Gallagher

Our journey of life is about progress,
     not perfection.
It's not about doing one thing
     100 percent better —
it's a matter of doing 100 things,
     one percent better each day.

Progress is evolutionary
     not revolutionary,
and most days we measure our progress
     in inches,
          not miles.

What matters most
     is showing up for your life
          whether you feel like it
               or not.

Ask yourself,
   "What two or three little things
      can I do today
      that would move me forward?"

You'll be amazed
   at how much distance
      you can cover
   by taking it in increments.

The little things add up;
      the inches turn to miles;
   and we string together our efforts
      like so many pearls.
Before long,
      look what you have —
      a whole strand!

   Ah … beautiful.

Patience, persistence, and perspiration make an **unbeatable combination** for success.

• Napoleon Hill, author of *Think and Grow Rich*

Tips for Tough Times

Sometimes we get so focused on how far we have to go that we can't see how far we've come.

Where you are today is the result of tens of thousands of decisions, actions and accomplishments.

Take a look back at your life thus far. *Make a list of the things you feel good about, no matter how small.*

Acknowledge yourself for the progress you've made.

You're on the path — that's what counts!

Ultimately, man should not ask what the meaning of his life is, but rather must recognize that it is he who is asked. In a word, **each man is questioned by life;** and he can only answer to life by answering for his own life. To life he can only respond by being responsible.

• Viktor E. Frankl, Austrian psychiatrist, author of *Man's Search for Meaning*

How do you get through tough times?

P
E
R
S
E
V
Embrace adversity as your teacher.
R
E

Finding Meaning in Suffering

None of us will ever face the depth of suffering witnessed and experienced by Viktor Frankl during World War II after he, his wife, and parents were deported to Theresianstadt concentration camp in Nazi Germany. There, he came face to face with despair, depression and death on a daily basis. He saw what happened when prisoners gave up hope. He noted the differences between those who maintained a strong will to live and those who lost theirs.

Frankl concluded that even in the most absurd, painful and dehumanized situation, life has meaning and that therefore even suffering is meaningful. This insight later became the basis for Frankl's development of a whole new form of existential analysis — logotherapy — "the will to meaning."

In the two years he spent at Theresianstadt, Frankl worked in the camp clinic, first serving as a general practitioner, then as a camp psychiatrist, organizing a special unit to help new arrivals overcome their shock and grief. It was forbidden to actively stop someone from committing suicide, so Frankl and others worked clandestinely to try to prevent their fellow prisoners from killing themselves.

In order to maintain his own mental health, Frankl reports that he would frequently march outside and deliver lectures to an imaginary audience about "The Psychotherapeutic Experiences in a Concentration Camp." He believed that by fully experiencing the suffering objectively, he would thereby end it.

After two years in Theresianstadt, he was transported to Auschwitz, and then to Türkheim, not far from Dachau. Frankl's wife was transferred to Bergen-Belsen concentration camp where she died; his parents had been sent to Auschwitz where they died as well.

In the Spring of 1945, Frankl was liberated by the Americans. Later that year, fresh from his horrific experience, he wrote his world-famous book. The title, translated from German, was: *Saying Yes to Life in Spite of Every-thing: A Psychologist's Experience of the Concentration Camp.* In English it was published as *Man's Search for Meaning.*

Frankl's experience in the hell of the Holocaust enabled him to plumb the depths of important existential questions, and through his work after the war, share his discoveries with others. He went on to publish more than thirty books; he taught seminars and lectured all over the world; and he was awarded 29 honorary doctorate degrees.

His contribution to the world is probably best summarized in his own words:

"We must never forget that we may also find meaning in life even when confronted with a hopeless situation, when facing a fate that cannot be changed. For what then matters is to bear witness to the uniquely human potential at its best, which is to transform a personal tragedy into a triumph, to turn one's predicament into a human achievement."

It's difficult in times like these; ideals, dreams and cherished hope rise within us, only to be crushed by grim reality. It's a wonder I haven't abandoned all my ideals, they seem so absurd and impractical. Yet I cling to them because I believe, in spite of everything, that **people are truly good at heart.** I simply can't build up my hopes on a foundation consisting of confusion, misery and death.

• Ann Frank, German Jewish girl who died in the Nazi death camps, *The Diary of Ann Frank* was published after the war was over

When we do the best that we can, **we never know what miracle** is wrought, in our life or in the life of another.

• Helen Keller, the first deaf blind person to earn a college degree

A broken spirit is more
disabling than a broken body.

• Roger Crawford, the first athlete with four
impaired limbs to compete in collegiate tennis

Success is how **high you bounce** when you hit bottom.

• General George S. Patton, legendary Army leader in WWII

PAIN

by BJ Gallagher

Someone wise once told me:

"Pain is the touchstone

of all spiritual growth."

If that's true,
then I must be
almost a saint by now.

To fly, we have to have **resistance.**

• Maya Ying Lin, architect who designed the Vietnam Veterans Memorial in Washington, DC

Every new day begins with possibilities. **It's up to us** to fill it with the things that move us toward progress and peace.

• Ronald Reagan, 40th President of the United States

Tips for Tough Times

How can you survive catastrophe?
How do you move through unthinkable loss and
unbearable pain?
Where do you find the strength to carry on?

Viktor Frankl suggests that each of us must find
something outside ourselves, something bigger than
we are, something significant and meaningful in order
for us to go on. For some it is family; for others it is
work; for still others it is their art; for many it is God.

What do you live for?
Why are you here?
What is the meaning you find in your life?

Spend some time reflecting and/or writing about
these questions.
They may help you through your own suffering.

It matters if you
don't give up.

• Stephen Hawking,
British theoretical physicist,
considered to be the greatest
mind in physics since Einstein

How do you get through tough times?

PERSEVERE

efuse to give up.

Defying the Diagnosis

It was 1962. Stephen Hawking was just twenty-one years old when he received the awful news that would change his life — he had amyotrophic lateral sclerosis (ALS), also known as Lou Gehrig's Disease. It's a devastating diagnosis: the disease is progressive, incurable and fatal. His doctors told him he had just a few years to live.

At the time, Hawking was a doctoral student at Cambridge, having already earned a degree from Oxford. But his research hadn't been going well; he was unmotivated in his work and bored with his life. His diagnosis was a turning point: he could either give up his studies and wait to die, or he could make the most of what time he had left. At first, he chose the road of despair and resignation. He wanted to give up because he didn't see any point in finishing his degree if he was going to die soon.

But he didn't give up for long. Through the encouragement and love of his girlfriend, Jane, he pulled out of his despair and found the fire and determination that had been missing before his diagnosis. He married Jane in 1965, finished his studies, and got a job at a university. True, he was afraid of dying, but even more, he was afraid that he would die without achieving anything in his life.

Hawking and Jane had three children together, and she devotedly cared for him year after year as his disease progressed. While his body was deteriorating, his career was blossoming. He was elected as one of the youngest Fellows of the Royal Society in 1974, became a Commander of the Order of the British Empire in 1982, and became a Companion of Honour in 1989. These acknowledgements and public honors were bestowed on Hawking for his contributions to the fields of theoretical cosmology and quantum gravity, especially in the context of black holes. He has published hundreds of research papers, as well as six books. His runaway bestseller was *A Brief History of Time,* which stayed on the Sunday Times best-seller list for a record-breaking 237 weeks — unheard of for a science book.

It's been over forty years since Hawking got his diagnosis from the doctors. He defied their prediction of an early death, as well as his early impulse to give up. Now completely paralyzed, wheelchair-bound and compelled to use a computer voice synthesizer, he is a respected scientist, a world-renowned celebrity and an inspiration to millions.

In a 2005 interview Hawking said, "It is a waste of time to be angry about my disability. One has to get on with life and I haven't done badly. People won't have time for you if you are always angry or complaining."

That's not a bad credo to live by.

You may not realize it when it happens, but **a kick in the teeth** may be the best thing in the world for you.

• Walt Disney, founder of Disneyland

Live as if you would die tomorrow.
Learn as if you were to live forever.

• Mahatma Gandhi, the Father of India, who led his country to independence from Britain through non-violence and truth

Everything can be taken from a man but ... the last of the human freedoms – **to choose one's attitude** in any given set of circumstances, to choose one's own way.

• Viktor Frankl, Austrian psychiatrist, Holocaust survivor, author of *Man's Search for Meaning*

No
Surrender

by BJ Gallagher

When you believe in yourself,
in your personal potential,
in your own future,
you have no choice —
surrender is not an option.
There's nothing to do
but continue.

Sometimes you want to give up,
but you can't —
something deep Inside
won't let you.

No white flags,
no bailing out,
no throwing in the towel
for you.

You have to keep going;
you must carry on;
you just take the next step …
and the next …
and the next …

You will face obstacles.
You will be blown off
the path, but because
you have a goal, you
stay on your path.

• Heather Whitestone, deaf since age two, she became
the first person with a disability to be crowned Miss America

Tips for Tough Times

Where do you get your stamina?

**Some people find it in their goals and dreams;
others draw on their love of family and friends;
some rely on spiritual sources.**

Explore and discover your own personal wellspring of stamina that keeps you going.

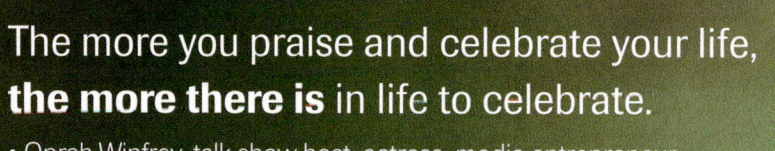

The more you praise and celebrate your life,
the more there is in life to celebrate.

• Oprah Winfrey, talk show host, actress, media entrepreneur

How do you get through tough times?

P
E
R
S
E
V
E
R
Enjoy and celebrate every tiny bit of progress!

"This I Know for Sure ..."

Born in 1954 to a poor, unmarried couple in rural Mississippi, Oprah Winfrey did not have much going for her. Her mother, Vernita Lee, was a housemaid and her father, Vernon Winfrey, was a coal miner. The teenage couple broke up after Vernita got pregnant.

After Oprah's birth, Vernita went north to live with her mother, Hattie Mae Lee. They were so poor that Oprah's grandmother clothed the child in dresses made of potato sacks, which made her the object of merciless teasing from the local kids. Grandma Hattie Mae was a powerful influence in young Oprah's life, teaching her to read by the time she was three, taking her to church every Sunday, and encouraging her to memorize and recite Bible verses. Hattie Mae was also a strict disciplinarian, taking a switch to the child if she misbehaved or didn't do her chores.

When Oprah was six, Vernita moved with Oprah to an inner-city neighborhood in Milwaukee, Wisconsin. The strong matriarchal presence of Hattie Mae was sorely missed, and young Oprah no longer had the support and discipline she needed. Her mother worked long hours as a maid, leaving her daughter to fend for herself.

To say that her home life was dysfunctional would be an understatement. At age nine, Oprah was molested by her cousin, her uncle and a family friend. As a young teen in the '60s, she rebelled and left home, choosing street life over her family. She became pregnant at 14, but her baby boy died shortly after birth. At this point, Vernita was so frustrated with her daughter that she sent her to live with her father, who was now a barber in Nashville, Tennessee.

Vernon Winfrey was strict, like her grandmother Hattie Mae had been. Oprah needed the structure and discipline her father provided, with an emphasis on education. Oprah blossomed into an honors student, was voted "most popular girl," and joined her high school speech team. She won an oratory contest, which enabled her to land a scholarship to Tennessee State University, a historically black college, where she studied communication. At seventeen, she won the title of Miss Black Tennessee, which caught the attention of the local black radio station, WVOL. The station manager hired the articulate, charming teen to do the news part-time.

And thus was born a media star — who would go on to work her way up through the radio and television business to become the richest, self-made woman in America.

Oprah credits her grandmother with being an important influence in her life, encouraging the child to speak in church. Hattie Mae "gave me a positive sense of myself," Oprah says.

She became a millionaire at age thirty-two when her daily talk show went into national syndication. At age forty-one, she replaced Bill Cosby as the only African American on the Forbes 400 Richest People in America. With a net worth over $2.5 billion, Forbes' international rich list cites Oprah as the first black woman billionaire in world history.

But she doesn't just make money — she gives it away. In 2005, Business Week listed Oprah as one of America's most generous philanthropists, having given away $303 million. In 2007, she spent $40 million and much of her time building and opening a girls' academy in South Africa. She has put 250 African American men through college. And she launched Oprah's Angel Network in 1998, to encourage young people around the world to make a difference to underprivileged others. Oprah covers all the administrative costs of the charity, so that 100% of the money raised — over $51 million to date — goes directly to the programs.

When asked about her secret to success, Oprah responds: "The big secret in life is that there is no big secret. Whatever your goal, you can get there if you're willing to work. ... My philosophy is that not only are you responsible for your life, but doing the best at this moment puts you in the best place for the next moment."

"Today is the first day of the rest of your life" is a bit portentous; I prefer to wake up to five-card-draw poker. Each morning, a new hand; some days, junk; some days, a full house; and every day, the challenge of **playing that hand to win.**

• Wendy Reid Crisp, author, magazine editor

Life is a succession of moments — to **live each one** is to succeed.

• Sister Corita Kent, artist

Celebration
by BJ Gallagher

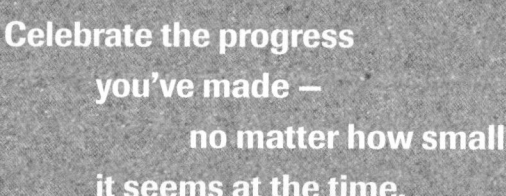

"Way to go!"
    "That's it!"
    "I knew you could do it!"
"Good for you!"
    "You've come a long way!"

Celebrate the progress
    you've made —
        no matter how small
    it seems at the time.

Success is not
    an all-or-nothing proposition —
    it's a thousand points of progress
        along the way.

Success is not just about winning —
it's about staying the course,
day in, day out.

Sometimes you're ahead,
sometimes you're running behind.
The most important thing is
you're on the field.

You can't win the Game of Life
if you're sitting in the bleachers.

History has demonstrated that the most notable winners usually encountered heartbreaking obstacles before they triumphed.
They won because **they refused to become discouraged** by their defeats.

• B.C. Forbes, publisher

If we all did the things we are capable of, we would **astound** ourselves.

• Thomas Edison, scientist, inventor of the light bulb and the phonograph

Tips for Tough Times

Catch yourself doing something right — and celebrate!

Instead of focusing on your faults and mistakes, turn your attention instead to the good things you do.

Pat yourself on the back when you take a positive step in the right direction. Throw a party when you reach a milestone. Look for ways to savor and celebrate your successes, both large and small.

Remember:
"Impossible"

means **"I'm possible."**

• SARK, artist, author

About the Author

BJ GALLAGHER

BJ Gallagher is an inspirational author, speaker, and storyteller. Her books, keynote speeches, and workshops are designed to educate, entertain, and enlighten people — consistently focusing on the "power of positive *doing*."

She has written nineteen books, including an international best-seller, *A Peacock in the Land of Penguins,* now published in 21 languages worldwide. Her other books include:

- *YES Lives in the Land of NO: A Tale of Triumph Over Negativity*
- *A True Friend … Is Someone Just Like You*
- *What Would Buddha do at Work?*
- *Everything I Need to Know I Learned from Other Women*

BJ is a much-in-demand keynote speaker, making frequent presentations at conferences and professional gatherings in the United States, Asia, Europe and Latin America. Her lively presentations inspire and instruct audiences of all types — with a style that is up-beat, fast-paced, funny, dynamic, and charismatic.

Her impressive client list includes: IBM, Chrysler Corporation, Southern California Edison, Los Angeles Times, Phoenix Newspapers Inc., American Press Institute, Atlanta Journal-Constitution, Raytheon, John Deere Credit, TRW, Farm Credit Services of America, U.S. Department of Interior, the American Lung Association, Chevron, Marathon Realty (Canada), and many others.

Visit BJ Gallagher's web sites:
www.yeslivesinthelandofno.com
www.bjgallagher.com
www.womenneed2know.com

Nothing in life just happens. You have to have the stamina to meet the obstacles and overcome them.

• Golda Meir, Fourth Prime Minister of Israel

If you have enjoyed this book we invite you to check out our entire collection of gift books, with free inspirational movies, at **www.simpletruths.com.** You'll discover it's a great way to inspire *friends* and *family,* or to thank your best *customers* and *employees.*

For more information, please visit us at:

www.simpletruths.com

Or call us toll free… **800-900-3427**